ABC, CAN YOU FIND ME?

Mill City Press, Inc.
2301 Lucien Way #415
Maitland, FL 32751
407.339.4217
www.millcitypress.net

Printed in the United States of America

ISBN-13: 9781545607107

OWLS AND BIRDS ON THIS BEAUTIFUL DAY.

CAN YOU FIND ALL THE A'S?

LOOK ALL AROUND. WHAT DO YOU SEE?

CAN YOU FIND ALL THE B'S?

DECORATIONS FILL THE TREE.

CAN YOU FIND ALL THE C'S?

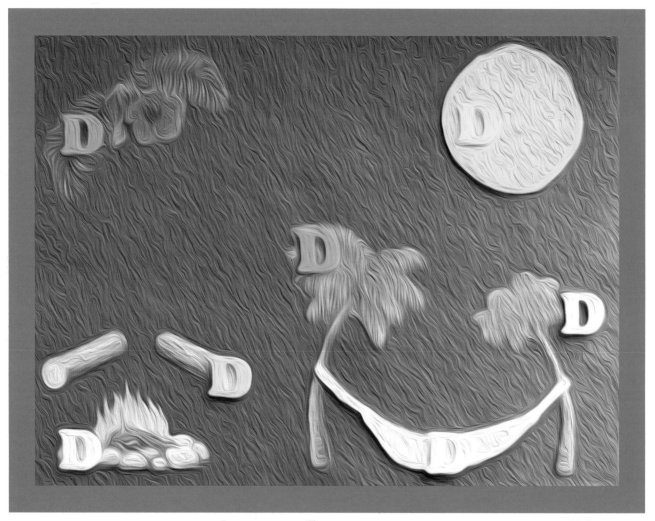

CAN YOU FIND ALL THE D's?

BUTTERFLIES FLYING HIGH AS CAN BE!

CAN YOU FIND ALL THE E'S?

WE'LL TAKE THESE VEGETABLES TO THE CHEF.

CAN YOU FIND ALL THE F'S?

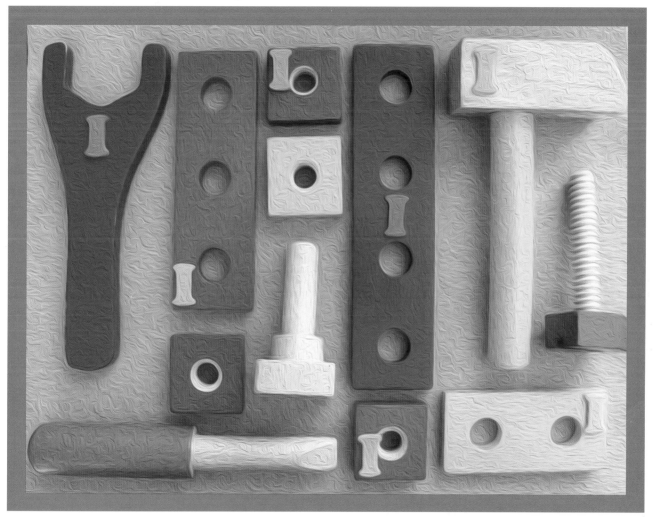

A LITTLE CANDY BEFORE WE PLAY!

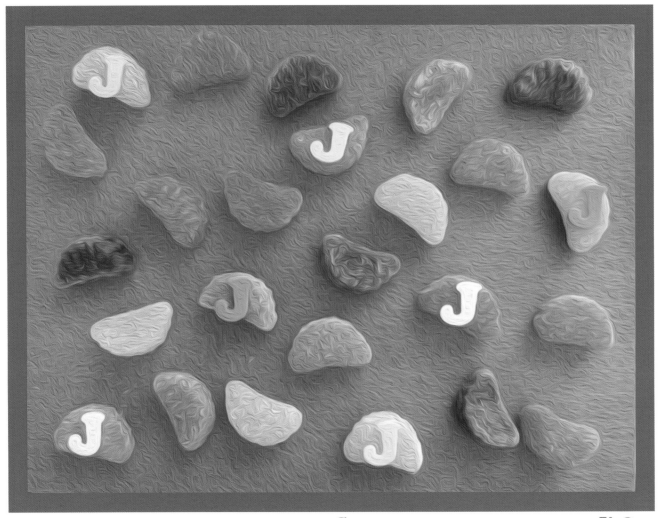

CAN YOU FIND ALL THE J'S?

CAN YOU FIND ALL THE L'S?

LITTLE BLOCKS, WHAT'S ON THEM?

CAN YOU FIND ALL THE M'S?

ON A WINDY DAY, THE LEAVES WILL BLOW.

CAN YOU FIND ALL THE O'S?

ALL THE ROCKS GO INTO MY JAR!

CAN YOU FIND ALL THE R's?

JUICY FRUITS CAN MAKE SOME MESSES!

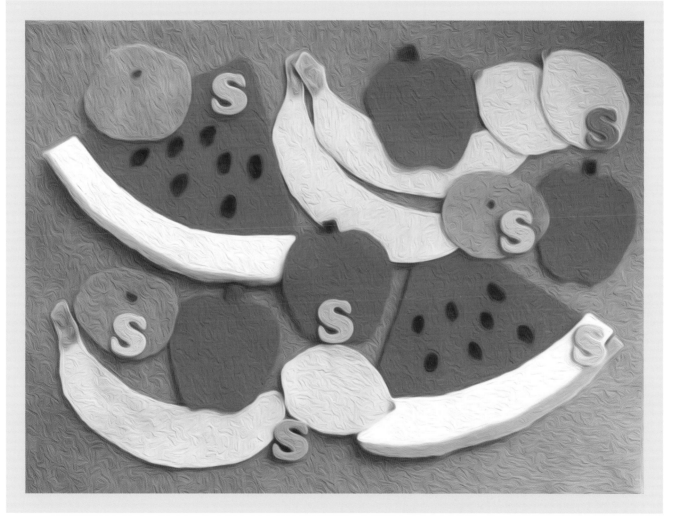

CAN YOU FIND ALL THE S'S?

A PRETTY PICTURE FOR YOU TO VIEW.

CAN YOU FIND ALL THE U's?

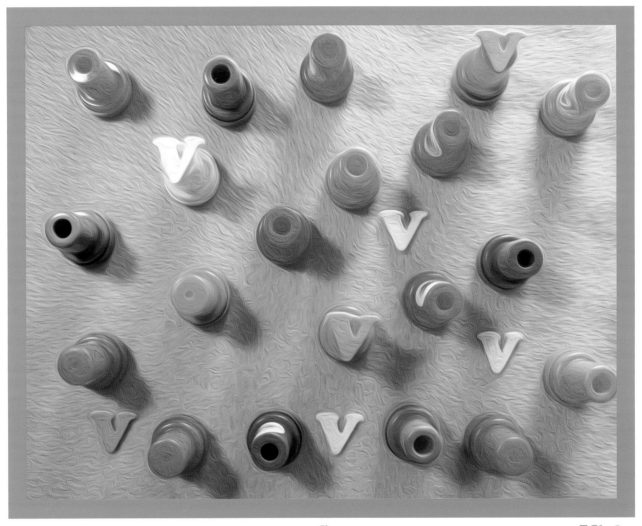

LOTS OF COLORS AND SHAPES TO SPY!

CAN YOU FIND ALL THE Y's?

CAN YOU FIND ALL THE Z'S?